8 Essential Values for Academic Leaders: A Quality Management Checklist

by

Joshua T. Fischer, Ph.D.

A Product of

and

Copyright © 2020 Joshua T. Fischer, Ph.D.

All rights reserved. In accordance with the U.S. Copyright Act of 1976, the scanning, uploading, and electronic sharing of any part of this book without the permission of the publisher constitute unlawful piracy and theft of the author's intellectual property. If you would like to use material from the book (other than for review purposes), prior written permission must be obtained by contacting the publisher at the address below. Thank you for your support of the author's rights.

Progressus Press
13517 E 93rd St N.
Owasso, OK 74055
ProgressusEd.com

Front & Back cover design by Bernell and Jeanna Clifford.

Printed by Ingram.

ISBN: 978-0-578-68107-8 (Paperback)
ISBN: 978-0-578-68118-4 (electronic book)

Library of Congress Catalog Card No. 2020907234

Printed in the Unites States of America.

Forward

Our God deserves our best. He is not interested in our sickly lambs, or less-than offerings. He goes as far as to say He is offended by them. He wants our best. Thankfully, not perfection, yet broken and contrite - in our best. Not because He needs anything from us, but because he wants us to obey Him and in that obedience we learn to trust Him more deeply.

That is the foundational principle driving my friend Dr. Joshua Fischer's recent work on quality management in higher education. In this coming era of unprecedented scrutiny of the academy, Dr. Fischer provides a helpful, practical and self-reflective rubric to consider how well we are doing as leaders in bringing God, our colleagues, and our students our very best in this arena of life mission.

> Dr. Peter W. Teague
> President Emeritus
> Lancaster Bible College/Capital Seminary &
> Graduate School

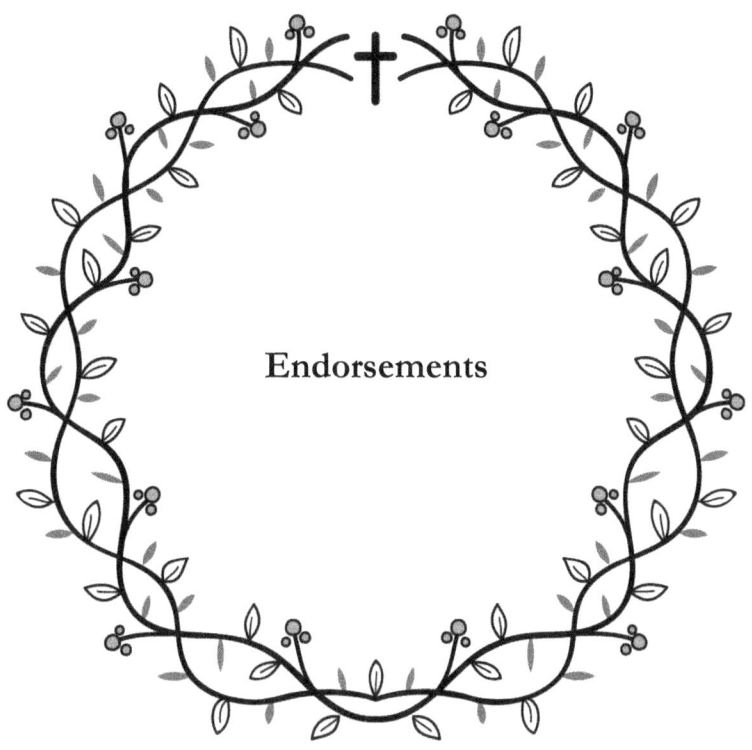

Endorsements

"Academic leaders in 2020 took on incredible new and unforeseen challenges. The very survival of Christian higher education now requires the highest levels of preparation and performance by leaders at all levels. Dr. Fischer's Quality Management outline is practical, challenging, linked to biblical truth, and will help prepare any leader in any organization for what lies ahead."

> Robert C. Andringa, Ph.D,
> President Emeritus
> Council for Christian Colleges & Universities

"Dr. Fischer's wealth of experience, commitment to educational excellence, and unquestionable love for Christ and His people position him as one of today's most reliable authorities in the world of Christian higher education. Christian administrators and educators seeking to more effectively oversee and administer God's work would do well to read and re-read his book, "8 Essential Values for Academic Leaders".

> Dr. Ron Cannon
> VP of Operations (COO)
> Transnational Association of Christian Colleges and Schools

"Dr. Joshua Fischer captures the core of what it means to be an effective Christian leader in higher education today. This book eloquently binds together biblical principles with key quality management values that moves the reader towards action. Dr. Fischer speaks from many years of experience as seen through multiple real-life leadership examples. Most helpful are the end-of-chapter assessments, checklists, and reflection opportunities to put into action sound principles. You won't want to rush through this helpful resource!"

>Philip E. Dearborn, Ed.D.
>President
>Association for Biblical Higher Education

Table of Contents

Forward 1

Endorsements 5

Introduction 13

The What and Why of QM for the Academic Leader 19

Vocational Certainty 25
    Definition & Discussion 27
    Scriptural Basis & Devotional 31
    Self-Assessment 35
    Institutional Checklist of To Dos 37
    Reflection 38

Process Quality 41
    Definition & Discussion 43
    Scriptural Basis & Devotional 47
    Self-Assessment 49
    Institutional Checklist of To Dos 51
    Reflection 52

Administrative Consistency 55
    Definition & Discussion 57
    Scriptural Basis & Devotional 61
    Self-Assessment 63
    Institutional Checklist of To Dos 65
    Reflection 66

Executive Credibility 69
    Definition & Discussion 71
    Scriptural Basis & Devotional 75
    Self-Assessment 77
    Institutional Checklist of To Dos 79

  Reflection 80

Personal Authenticity..83
  Definition & Discussion 85
  Scriptural Basis & Devotional...................................89
  Self-Assessment 91
  Institutional Checklist of To Dos..............................93
  Reflection 94

Ethical Dependability 97
  Definition & Discussion 99
  Scriptural Basis & Devotional.................................103
  Self-Assessment 107
  Institutional Checklist of To Dos............................109
  Reflection 110

KTP Culture..113
  Definition & Discussion 115
  Scriptural Basis & Devotional.................................119
  Self-Assessment 123
  Institutional Checklist of To Dos............................125
  Reflection 126

Zero Defects Attitude...129
  Definition & Discussion 131
  Scriptural Basis & Devotional.................................135
  Self-Assessment 137
  Institutional Checklist of To Dos............................139
  Reflection 140

Assessment Review & Reflection 143

Next Steps 149

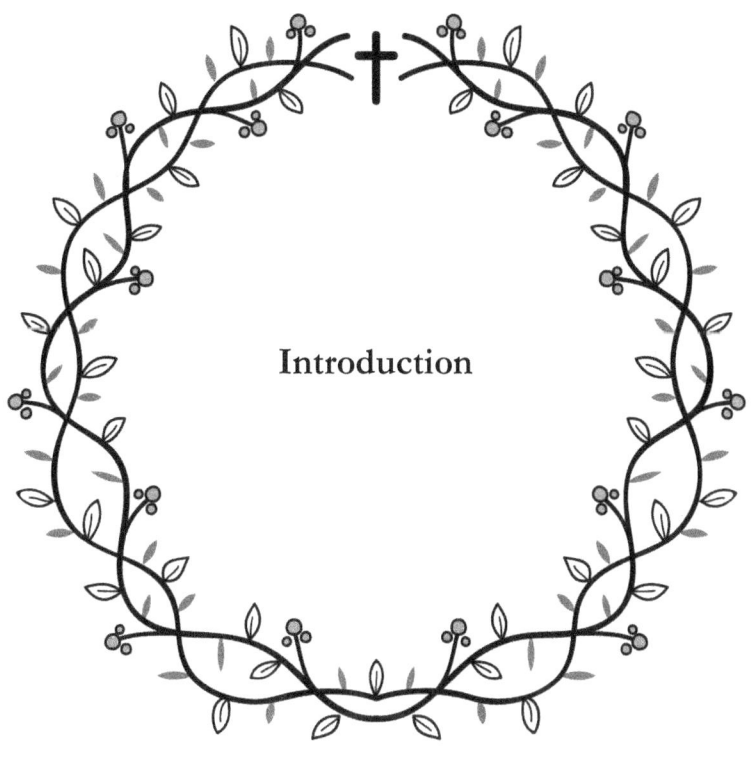

Introduction

I began this book as a devotional because of its Biblical focus on the concepts within Quality Management. After a dear friend and colleague read the manuscript, he suggested it was more of a checklist or inventory. I decided he was correct. I hope this will serve as a resource to guide you in getting the right things done in your personal and higher education endeavors.

My career in higher education has ranged from a professor to more than 9,000 students, to a program director, to a dean, to a college president. I have felt a strong calling in each of those varied roles.

I now head InterLearn (www.InterLearnEd.com), a higher education consulting company, which assists program leaders to move learning into online and adult formats. I also lead a quality management training and consulting company, Progressus (www.ProgressusEd.com), as a result of my relationship with the Quality Management Institute (QMI).

This book was born from my desire to connect the values of my Christian faith and higher education administration with the quality management learned through Quality Management Institute's Certified Quality Manager training program. The values are compatible, as you will see.

This book covers the eight quality manager values outlined by the Quality Management Institute. Progressus has gained permission to develop this resource based on the material from QMI's training. The views, opinions, and perspectives, however, are not necessarily the same as those shared by QMI.

There will be a dual focus, description and action, on each of the eight values. The description section will define each value so that you understand the concept. Then, I will show the Biblical perspective in a devotional format. From there, it will be time for you to take action.

You will have the opportunity for a self-assessment of your academic and administrative practices as well as your personal habits. After the assessment, there will be a checklist of quality habits to add to your personal and institutional practices. These habits are related to the specific value being discussed in that section. Additionally, there will be space to reflect on what you have learned from our description section and your self-assessment.

These eight quality management values are divided into several types: Vocational values, Personal values, Keeping the Promise Culture, and Zero Defects Attitude. Vocational values focus on work life, while personal values are broader. Keeping the Promise Culture is a concept that requires personal and organizational investment and the Zero Defects Attitude is at the heart of all quality management.

You may complete this book in eight hours, eight days, or even eight weeks. Use the timeline that allows you to thoroughly reflect on your own practice. After completing the study, there are some additional steps for you to consider.

You also may notice that I use "Biblical" instead of "biblical." I understand that the correct grammatical and typographical version of the word is lowercase. I have, however, always used "Biblical" as a means of honoring the Word of God.

I hope you find this book meaningful to your spiritual walk and to your daily practices within your academic work.

    Joshua

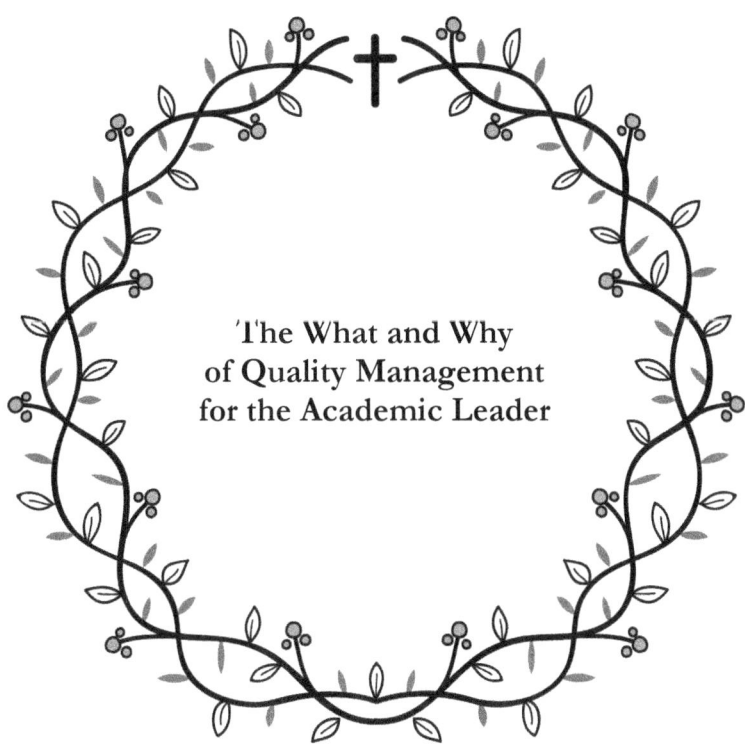

The What and Why of Quality Management for the Academic Leader

I have had two distinct perspectives on higher education during my career. I have been on the inside looking out as an academic (faculty, director, dean, and president). I have been on the outside looking in as a consultant. I have found fulfillment in the work I have done, and continue to do, since answering what I felt was my call to higher education.

The joy of seeing results in higher education, in general, are magnified for those of us who are blessed to practice our profession in a Christian setting. The ability to change the trajectory of a person's life through learning is profound. The implications of Christian higher education, of course, have eternal ramifications when used to reach people with the message of salvation.

Despite my love for higher education, I still see problems in the field. I want to pinpoint some of those problems, which I believe we are failing to address.

There is a common misconception that higher education programs and institutions are of optimal quality merely because they are accredited. While that process is supposed to show evidence of quality, too often it does not. Accreditation can and does offer credible evidence that an institution meets the quality thresholds and characteristics established by the agency. Additionally, in recent years, governmental and professional recognition of accrediting agencies is based on the idea that institutions they accredit have established rigorous ongoing assessment, planning, and improvement processes.

Accreditation, however, has significant weaknesses when it comes to ensuring that all institutional units and processes operate at the highest possible level of quality. There are multiple reasons. One is the magnitude and breadth of accrediting agency oversight responsibility. Even if the agencies could keep up with the demand, they are unable, through periodic peer evaluator reviews, to delve deeply enough into an institution's practice to fully understand all the aspects of the institution. I say this with respect and sympathy for accreditors, having been a peer reviewer as well as worked for an accrediting body early in my career. Accreditation teams do their best, but they are unable to keep up and get the full picture.

From an institutional perspective, accreditation is seen as an event, not a process. It can turn into a paper job with no real impact on the quality of the organization and its personnel. I know of colleges that designed their accreditation process for the site visit with no disclosure of what is happening at the institution. This is fraud and has even more frightening Biblical implications at a Christian institution. When a college is not doing what it is saying, it is lying.

Another issue is the idea that non-profit and Christian higher education institutions do not have to make a profit. The thought is that money to cover the budget will magically appear because the institution has a program. Sadly, excellent Christian institutions are regularly closed because a misunderstanding of the non-profit concept led to empty coffers. Instead of wisely stewarding finances to accomplish the mission and vision, leaders spend without considering the consequences. As one astute colleague said, "Where there is no margin, there is no mission."

Perhaps the most grievous concern in Christian higher education is the idea that goodness is good enough. We all have good intentions. We consider it ministry of the highest order, a sacred calling, and nothing less than a quality education will do. Too often, however, our goal of having quality programming is sacrificed in our pursuit of goodness. Quality education must deliver much more.

In non-profits, especially, the mission drives the organization. But when goodness or good intentions becomes the excuse for failure, out goes quality. "Oh, Joe meant well. I know he caused us to lose the students but his heart was in the right place." "Karen had good intentions when she overspent the budget for the program." "We should not let Tim go because of his regular mistakes. He tries to do the right thing. Yes, we have told him he needs to do better, but he reminds us how his intention is to follow the mission."

To put it bluntly, "Your Goodness is not Good Enough." Your best intentions, your plans, reputation, mission and vision statements, course objectives, annual goals, strategic plans and knowledge of the situation are not good enough. If you excuse poor performance because intentions are good, you have let down the institution's founders and those who lead the organization today with that same mission and vision. Goodness is not good enough.

This is where quality management (or QM) is key. "Quality management is an educational technology with systems, methods and language (that) help us reach our business and organizational goals" (Kennedy, n.d.). Within the non-profit organization, QM encourages development of practices that produce extra reserves to accomplish new aspects of the organizational mission, carry the organization during times of lower income, and help the leadership care for employees and those the ministry serves.

I believe, based on my research and experience, that it is imperative to pursue quality management. In fact, quality may be the death knell to the Christian college. While there is concern about agendas that violate most Christian college theological perspectives, those institutions may get a pass for a while. What they will not get past is a lack of quality. If colleges are producing subpar products, students who are poorly educated due to poor quality programming, no one will stand up for this form of Christian higher education.

So, the key to quality management for the academic leader is to stem the tide of these issues. We are about a holy calling in Christian higher education, but we must seek practices that raise the quality of the education we deliver and of the organizations we operate. Leaving quality up to accreditation will only continue the downward slide of quality in our education and our organizations.

References

Kennedy, L. (n.d.). *QM and profitability*. [Online video]. Available from http://www.qualitymanagementinstitute.com

1

Vocational Certainty

Vocational Certainty
Definition & Discussion

In quality management terms, vocational certainty is a value regarding your work life. Vocationally certain individuals have the training and education, talents, skill sets, emotional maturity, and willingness to perform their work with excellence. The vocationally certain are always furthering their skills to manage their responsibilities.

Within most organizations, we can think of individuals who are not vocationally certain. Workers at all levels enter roles for which they are not prepared. They lack the talent to lead people, manage budgets, etc. They are emotionally unstable and unwilling to prepare themselves to work with excellence. People who whine about working conditions are probably lacking in vocational certainty.

In higher education, we hope our team members will have vocational certainty. We are usually highly educated, but formal education does not always mean that the necessary training and education are in place. This begins often at the board level with people who have no board experience. As board members, they go along to get along instead of helping the leaders they have hired to be more effective. Board members, like other people in other roles, need development training. A weak board coupled with a weak leader is a recipe for disaster.

Too often, a leader is placed in a role to honor his or her accomplishment in another area without any training for the new role. For example, a retired pastor is named president of a college but has neither the educational administrative knowledge nor the organizational understanding for what is a very complex job. I know of one denomination that requires its college presidents to have denominational ministry credentials. Regrettably, this denomination has faced successive failures, which led to the closure of some of its institutions because of ineffective leadership. Being a minister does not automatically prepare you for educational administration. In some cases, there have been success stories. However, in those cases, the minister continued to grow and learn.

Vocational certainty is not just a need for top leaders. It is needed at every level. When workers are not equipped for a role, are not emotionally mature, refuse to work with excellence, and will not grow and learn, leaders need to recognize that those workers are not vocationally certain. Astute leadership will either help those people grow or find a role that matches their vocational certainty (which may be outside the organization).

When I held an interim role at an institution, we had a vacancy for a student services role. We had a well-liked team member who was doing a great job in another position, but he felt he needed to make more money. The student services role was a higher level and paid better. Given his reputation and his need, we approved the transfer and hired him. What we did not factor in very well was his vocational certainty. He had no real experience in student services, no training in the area, and no educational administration background. While we trained him to do the work, he was unable to make the transition effectively. He could not get control of the duties of the role and was failing to do the work. After repeated efforts to help him, we recognized that he could not do the required work. Since his previous position was no longer available, he was terminated. We had not sufficiently appreciated the impact of his vocational uncertainty in the new position, nor his unwillingness or inability to learn it well and perform with excellence.

New faculty members who join the higher education ranks lack vocational certainty as teachers. They may be gifted to teach, but rarely have been *trained* to teach in their academic training. As a result, new faculty members must be helped to develop their vocational certainty in the classroom as a teacher. They will not automatically have the skillsets needed to teach. Academic leaders <u>must</u> recognize this and provide the necessary development to help new faculty perform with excellence. Seasoned faculty also must continue to grow or they will lose their relevance. Whether it is generational understanding, new field information, technology, or changes to standards of the institution, faculty members must continue to develop their vocational certainty.

Lack of vocational certainty becomes clear to those in the institution, to the students, and to those in the community when they come in contact with people who do not have it. The missing ingredient in their practice will produce undesired results that are striking. Leaders must see that people lacking in vocational certainty have opportunities to develop their skills and perform with excellence in an emotionally mature way or help them find their way into a new role within (or outside) the institution.

Vocational Certainty
Scriptural Basis & Devotional

> *But the wisdom that comes from heaven is first of all pure; then peace-loving, considerate, submissive, full of mercy and good fruit, impartial and sincere.*
>
> James 3:17 (NIV)

Vocational Certainty is a measure of your faithfulness to your agenda which includes your work priorities, job description, and career path. The Bible has so much to say about the topic of faithfulness. Not only is it a characteristic of our Creator, it is a characteristic that He desires to see in us, His followers.

Jesus, in Luke 12, talks to His disciples about remaining faithful and ready:

> *The Lord answered, "Who then is the faithful and wise manager, whom the master puts in charge of his servants to give them their food allowance at the proper time? It will be good for that servant whom the master finds doing so when he returns. Truly I tell you, he will put him in charge of all his possessions. (vs 42-44)* (NIV)

In I Corinthians 4:2, Paul is talking about the requirements of his vocation in ministry. If our work is our service to God, regardless of the field, then the scripture applies to all work:

> *Now it is required that those who have been given a trust must prove faithful.* (NIV)

As we consider the vocation to which we are called, or those steps in between, we must be faithful to the work before us.

Our chosen vocation is central to the fulfillment of our human desires for life, family, personal achievement, and spiritual growth. So, it follows that nothing could be more relevant to developing our vision for our life and our profession than to have a clear understanding of our vocational strengths and weaknesses. We can remedy some weaknesses by acquiring knowledge, skills, etc., but other weaknesses might be indicators that we are more suited for profession "B" than profession "A." Conversely, strengths can be milestones that help define a reliable route toward fulfilling our hopes and dreams.

To be sure that we are pursuing the right agenda, we should judge the validity of our vision through the lens of some important questions.

Do I have a sense of intellectual integrity about this idea? Are the thoughts and motives that are energizing me pure before God? Are my plans really clear? Do my gifts and talents naturally support what I am considering?

Do I have a clear moral conscience about this plan? Am I at peace and are the steps I have taken producing peace in me? Or, do I really feel uneasy but have pushed on because I want something more than I should?

Am I being faithful to the task? Are my actions reasonable when I take steps to fulfill my objective or do I find myself becoming unreasonably aggressive? Am I forcing things to happen as opposed to gently and carefully stewarding my responsibilities?

Am I making a reasonable judgment? Is this plan reasonable? Does it pass the test of common sense or am I rationalizing facts and events? When I consider giving up, do I feel peaceful and free, and exhibit the "fruit" of God's Spirit, or do I feel angry and desperate? Is there any wavering within me, or hypocrisy in what I am considering? Am I really speaking truth to myself or is there conflict in my heart?

These are the difficult questions that must be asked. If they are not asked and answered, we could find ourselves making bad decisions and discover too late that our vision is critically flawed.

Vocational Certainty
Self-Assessment

Using the scoring scale, rate each area of the question. At the end of the Assessment, tally the score by letter (i.e. tally the totals for A, B, and C, separately).

On a scale of 1 to 5, where 1 is Never, 2 is Hardly Ever, 3 is Some of the Time, 4 is Most of the Time, and 5 is All of the Time,

1) How often is each group equipped to do the work they are assigned (through skills, education, talents, gifts):
    A. Each of the leaders in the organization?
    B. Each of the team members in your area?
    C. You?
2) How often does each group act emotionally mature:
    A. Each of the leaders in the organization?
    B. Each of the team members in your area?
    C. You?
3) How often does each group perform with excellence:
    A. Each of the leaders in the organization?
    B. Each of the team members in your area?
    C. You?
4) How often does each group continue to develop the skills needed to manage processes within their responsibility areas:
    A. Each of the leaders in the organization?
    B. Each of the team members in your area?
    C. You?

	Place your response for each question in the appropriate cell. Total the columns in the "T" row at the bottom.		
	Total of A Leaders in the Organization	Total of B Team Members in your Area	Total of C You
1			
2			
3			
4			
T			

Vocational Certainty
Institutional Checklist of To Dos

Incorporate these items into the practice of your institution to engage in this QM Value:

- ☐ Hire for Vocational Certainty.
- ☐ Review for Vocational Certainty.
- ☐ Develop Vocational Certainty in:
    - The Board
    - The President
    - The Chief Executives
    - The Administrative Team
    - The Faculty
    - Your Constituencies:
        - Students (of course)
        - Alumni
        - Donors
        - Community
- ☐ Remove Whiners from the Team.
- ☐ Require Team Members to Perform with Excellence.

Vocational Certainty Reflection

2

Process Quality

Process Quality
Definition & Discussion

Process quality is another vocational value within quality management. Developing the plans and budgeting resources to accomplish the plan are vital in providing products and/or services that are beneficial and consistent for the customer. That is process quality. Without it, results are not replicable, and quality is not consistent.

A quality leader must work to determine the facts of the situation. Process quality is about collecting those facts through effective planning and budgeting that is rational and unbiased. For the quality leader, it is not about being right; it is about finding the right solution by submitting biases to a process.

There are many leaders in higher education who have grand ideas of leading a powerful institution to greatness and fame. Regrettably, without the ability to develop plans and submit to the disciplines required for process quality, fame and greatness will never arrive. Every election cycle, politicians propose grand plans, but without process quality none of those plans become part of their legacy. One leader I know is recognized for his vision for higher education, which is the thing that I most admire about him. He has come to realize that he can have great vision, but if he does not submit it to the process of developing the plans and counting the cost, none of it will come to fruition. He and his teamwork to develop plans that will accomplish the vision with activities and budgets to match the plans. Leaders who expect things to happen without process quality end up shaken when their institution finds itself failing.

As a practical application of process quality in higher education, imagine starting a degree program without a plan or budget. Without the plan, students would not know the courses in the program, the costs for the program, or what would be gained from completing the program. The faculty would be confused concerning what should be taught, who would teach it, and how it would be assessed. Without the plan, state and accreditation approvals are out of the question. Process quality is what most accreditors are looking at in their visits and document reviews. Without going through steps to develop plans and budgets, you would not have the answers and the process would never be completed. Maintaining process quality requires you and your team to understand what needs to happen for a good outcome (product, service, building).

At most places I have served, I regularly submitted proposals for what we needed to do as an institution. I continue to do it for my clients. In some cases, these proposals were (and are) long due to the level of detail required. One of my proposals was not clear enough for those not deeply invested in the process. My vice president looked it over and shook his head. He looked up, smiled, and said something to this effect, "This is dizzying to try to understand and put into action." (To his credit, he did this in private and in a tone of developing and challenging me to do better.) The quality of the process was neither clear enough nor high enough to be effective. Yet even his negative feedback was necessary because it informed me how to improve and how to do better with future proposals.

In a more successful proposal, I worked with my team to design a process and plan to recruit faculty. We took a process that had been used for years and made it more understandable by developing start-to-finish steps. Since our institution had many offsite locations (in office spaces and hotels) and campuses across several states, the faculty recruitment proposal was adopted for all of those sites. We implemented a quality process for the entire institution because we made it clear and consistent, based on good planning and information. With this success, we expanded from faculty recruiting to recommending other systems that created value.

Process quality is not limited to big-ticket items. It applies to the smallest level work happening within your organization. Even a mini version of process quality should be part of daily decisions. Many people end their day with a feeling that nothing was accomplished because of interruptions. Whether it is the telephone ringing, constant interruptions from coworkers, email arriving in their inbox, or something else, they wonder what they accomplished. "I remember I got to the office, at some point I grabbed lunch, and later I looked up and the day was over." That can be a frequent recollection of a day's work without process quality.

Instead of ignoring process quality, design your day around priorities you must accomplish. Keep checklists, set aside time to work on projects free of interruptions. Gather information you need to do the work. With all details in hand, develop the work product. I block off days in my calendar for writing and working on specific projects, and do not schedule meetings those days. I close my email, put my telephone on silent, and close my office door. If I really need to focus, I put a note on the door telling my children there is a to-do list waiting for them in my office if they disturb me. (Okay, I have not used this tactic, but I am saving it if I need it.)

As you become more adept at taking the process quality steps, you will naturally focus on making sure you cover all your bases. As you will see in the devotional, being diligent in even the smallest of processes keeps huge mistakes from happening.

Process Quality
Scriptural Basis & Devotional

Where there is no vision [no revelation of God and His word], the people are unrestrained; But happy and blessed is he who keeps the law [of God].
Proverbs 29:18 (AMP)

It is said that leaders must have a big vision to motivate their followers to action. That requires the complete unity of the team, a riveting focus on the objectives, and what the participants believe is a vision of, for, and from God. This may sound attractive to someone who has never had to lead people on what General George Patton once called a "desperate mission." But once you have struggled through the details of project management, the high-minded words, which initially described your vision, sound less heroic and romantic, even when you are successful.

What is more difficult is to find reality after a defeat, especially when you were sure it was a God thing. It is usually after a sobering moment that maturing leaders realize they would happily trade big, or exciting, or transformative for words such as real, reliable, accurate, and achievable.

Sometimes we find ourselves rushing past the facts to achieve an outcome. In a world of agile and lean concepts, the due diligence, rigor, and systems thinking that create reliable processes can be unwisely ignored. When that happens, we find a sobering and sometimes terrifying awakening that awaits our arrival at the limits of our abilities.

The law of God is more than moral, ethical, and spiritual dogma. It is full of values, principles, and methodologies that will guide those who keep or follow. It will help them discover a bad idea disguised as a good one. This bad comes to mind as a flash of exciting vision but proves to be less than doable. Alternatively, we can discover that facts provide a basis for wisdom and adjustments to help us avoid failure and turn a potentially sad learning experience into a success.

Process Quality
Self-Assessment

Using the scoring scale, rate each area of the question. At the end of the Assessment, tally the score by letter (i.e. tally the totals for A, for B, and C, separately).

On a scale of 1 to 5, where 1 is Never, 2 is Hardly Ever, 3 is Some of the Time, 4 is Most of the Time, and 5 is All of the Time,

1) How often are strategic plans developed and shared to accomplish organizational level goals by:
    A. Each of the leaders in the organization?
    B. Each of the team members in your area?
    C. You?
2) How often are strategic plans developed and shared to accomplish departmental or project goals or general work processes by:
    A. Each of the leaders in the organization?
    B. Each of the team members in your area?
    C. You?
3) How often are budgets developed and actually used for the organization at large by:
    A. Each of the leaders in the organization?
    B. Each of the team members in your area?
    C. You?
4) How often are budgets developed and actually used for individual projects by:
    A. Each of the leaders in the organization?
    B. Each of the team members in your area?
    C. You?

	Place your response for each question in the appropriate cell. Total the columns in the "T" row at the bottom.		
	Total of A Leaders in the Organization	Total of B Team Members in your Area	Total of C You
1			
2			
3			
4			
T			

Process Quality
Institutional Checklist of To Dos

Incorporate these items into the practice of your institution to engage in this QM Value:

- ☐ Require clear, fact-based proposals for new endeavors.
- ☐ Request support for positions individuals hold, especially when they are dubious.
- ☐ Develop process documents for each area of work in your institution.
- ☐ Break down the vision into well-thought-out, researched plans that can be accomplished through reliable, strategic plans.
- ☐ Remember that economics control process and budget accordingly.

Process Quality Reflection

3

Administrative Consistency

Administrative Consistency
Definition & Discussion

A third vocational value in quality management is administrative consistency. This is a measure of attention to the details of your work, whether they are related to tasks, protocols and procedures, paperwork, or constituent requirements. A quality leader pays attention to those details to ensure the numbers are correct and the lists are complete and finished.

Listening to constituents—team members, students, donors, etc.—is vital because the institution cannot operate without their support. When leaders forge ahead without research and without listening to their members, they likely will not do enough to account for their own bias nor will they get necessary support.

Administrative consistency is critical in higher education. Our entire organization is supposed to be functioning based on data from assessment processes. Sadly, too many organizations fail to properly use their assessment data. Instead of setting up systems that collect useable data, they set up highly complex but useless assessment processes, never use the data collected – or both. The data are only embellished and used when preparing for an accreditation visit. I worked with one institution where a department created its assessment plan for a ten-year visit from the regional accreditor, but never consulted the plan again. The sigh of relief was, "Good! We don't need to do this for another ten years!"

Higher education leaders who do not follow up with the proper procedures of their organization or compliance bodies (such as state governments, accrediting bodies, financial aid, etc.) end up leading their organizations into significant turmoil. I have seen financial aid procedures not followed, retirement monies not placed into employee accounts, hiring procedures not observed, and student rights violated. In every case, attention to the data and procedures would have saved heartache and, in some cases, legal problems. By failing to follow established policies and procedures, we are acting fraudulently to our accreditors and constituents.

Some individuals, including me, are more detail oriented. It is sometimes all I can do to keep from mentioning missed details to those around me. There is, however, a fine balance between pointing out the details and knowing when to extend grace — awaiting the best time to share those details as a learning opportunity.

Then there are big-picture people who could not find a detail to save their lives. My brother, for example, has had to learn how to manage details in his career, and he has done that well. He now is a college professor and formerly worked in higher education administration. I know numerous top-level leaders who are big-picture people and struggle with the details. They have had to make sure details are effectively covered.

It is not that a person is detail-oriented and unable to see the big picture or have great vision. Or vice versa, that a person can see the big picture but cannot see the details. Rather, it is a *tendency*. Recognizing that you have a proclivity towards one or the other is important. If you identify with big-picture qualities, then you must be sure that details are covered. The danger arises when people let themselves off the hook because they are big-picture people. It can be an excuse that ends with negative consequences to their personal life, job, and, ultimately, to their employer.

Paying attention to the details of our work in higher education is not only the right thing to do, it pays exceptional dividends.

Administrative Consistency
Scriptural Basis & Devotional

It is the glory of God to conceal a matter; to search out a matter is the glory of kings.
Proverbs 25:2 (NIV)

It is possible to dread and either consciously or unconsciously resist completing the tasks that will bring clarity to a project and determine your path to success or failure. And if you hate administrative tasks, it is a good indicator that you might also be resisting other forms of personal or professional discipline that are essential to your success. Someone once said, "Having administrative duties to complete is often an indicator of prosperity." In other words, you would not have certain tasks to complete if your vision (or work-life) was failing. When your vision is sitting dead in the water without wind in your sails, you might long for those nasty administrative duties. The things that you have wrongly thought kept you entangled and away from the "creative" part of your work might just be the "mess in the cow's stall" that indicates something good . . . like productivity.

That is often the way it is with research and keeping lists of requirements that will define both the path and processes you need to be successful. Hebrews 12 tells us that

All discipline for the moment seems not to be joyful, but sorrowful; yet to those who have been trained by it, afterwards it yields the peaceful fruit of righteousness
Heb 12:11 (NIV)

It often seems as if God conceals a matter so we can endure the discipline required to seek out the matter and then enjoy the "peaceful fruit of righteousness" we gain by properly "enduring." Endurance is not the ability to survive and be robot-like in obedience through difficulties; it is an attribute of righteousness that is attained through practice, repetitions, re-enforcements, and the wisdom it produces.

To "search out a matter" has greater importance than just finding the right facts and getting the logistical or organizational attributes of your vision properly aligned. Of course, these are legitimate reasons to apply ourselves to research. But to follow the Biblical principles faithfully and with a believing heart, yields much greater dividends; not the least of which is a greater intimacy with God.

If we are organizational leaders or just individuals who are values-based and facts-driven, we require the emotional sobriety and rational stability to honestly evaluate our choices of path, methods, available resources, and, most importantly, what we believe is compatible with our faith.

In other words, the pursuit of reliable facts and perceptions through research together with the objective analysis of the facts and their impact on our faith is essential.

Administrative Consistency
Self-Assessment

Using the scoring scale, rate each area of the question. At the end of the Assessment, tally the score by letter (i.e. tally the totals for A, for B, and C, separately).

On a scale of 1 to 5, where 1 is Never, 2 is Hardly Ever, 3 is Some of the Time, 4 is Most of the Time, and 5 is All of the Time,

1) How often is attention given to the details of the work you do by
    A. Each of the leaders in the organization?
    B. Each of the team members in your area?
    C. You?
2) How often is care demonstrated for customer needs and job requirements from the customer by
    A. Each of the leaders in the organization?
    B. Each of the team members in your area?
    C. You?
3) How often is paperwork (reports, order forms, etc.) accurate from
    A. Each of the leaders in the organization?
    B. Each of the team members in your area?
    C. You?
4) How often are the proper protocols and procedures used by
    A. Each of the leaders in the organization?
    B. Each of the team members in your area?
    C. You?

	Place your response for each question in the appropriate cell. Total the columns in the "T" row at the bottom.		
	Total of A Leaders in the Organization	Total of B Team Members in your Area	Total of C You
1			
2			
3			
4			
T			

Administrative Consistency
Institutional Checklist of To Dos

Incorporate these items into the practice of your institution to engage in this QM Value:

- ☐ Follow established protocols.
- ☐ Pay attention to the details of organization:
  - o Dashboards
  - o Enrollment Numbers
  - o Attrition/Retention
  - o Budgets
  - o Employee Policies
  - o Student Policies
  - o Compliance Organizations
- ☐ Require accurate reports and paperwork.
- ☐ Prepare accurate reports and paperwork required for work you do.
- ☐ Focus on the details of your students and other constituents.

Administrative Consistency Reflection

4

Executive Credibility

Executive Credibility
Definition & Discussion

The final vocational value of quality management is executive credibility, which is a measure of skill and sincerity with people. As a quality leader, you must deal with people in order to accomplish your work. While many leaders are good at interacting with people in some areas, they are often missing a component or two.

To *have* executive credibility, you must commit yourself to practices that help you *be* credible. A leader with credibility talks with those inside and outside the organization. When an individual cannot discuss a topic using reason and avoiding bias, but instead resorts to coercion or manipulation, others cannot and will not rely on that person. Conversely, when a leader is known to be reasonable, that person is trusted, even when he or she has made a mistake. Others have confidence their leader will do the right thing and proceed to the best outcome. If you are a credible leader, you listen and show concern for others when you are conversing with them. No matter who you are interacting with and what you want done, you do not manipulate, push, or pressure. Instead, you explain what needs to be done and work with them to accomplish the tasks.

Lack of executive credibility in higher education is often easy to spot. There is the faculty member who connects poorly with students, either through arrogance or inept communication, by failing to clearly present information. One of my daughter's professors insisted he had presented the material well because "one person passed the test." (It was not my daughter who passed.) One student in the class passing the exam is not proof the faculty member has communicated well or has credibility with students. Rather, it demonstrates the individual is not a teacher, but is instead a Subject Matter Expert at best. Or you have administrators who are sure they are right, so they push and manipulate to defend their priorities. Then there is the president who does not appear to care about the wellbeing of his or her team. Leaders who fail to bring their team along with them or give them enough value and attention, will eventually lose the team's support.

Over the years, I have worked for people who lacked executive credibility. Sadly, several were top leaders who too often lashed out at others to make things happen. To avoid displays of anger, people complied to avoid ugly confrontation, future retribution, or immediate termination. When the leader shows this example, it becomes part of the culture and lieutenants within the organization begin to adopt those tactics. If regular outbursts of anger are your primary attribute, your executive credibility is non-existent. Then there are those leaders who engender distrust based on their history of manipulation. You are always wondering what their angle is when they talk to you.

A leader who is naturally sincere from the heart is one with executive credibility. "People do not care how much you know until they know how much you care," is a familiar adage. Sincerity will connect you to people better than facts and figures. Trust me, people know when you are being sincere or disingenuous.

Quality leaders improve their credibility by continually developing themselves and their skills. When you do things better, people around you will begin to notice your improved abilities. I have watched leaders go through education and training. When they use that training to grow, and not just put on airs because they have advanced their degree, it is amazing how people react to their new understanding. Personal development is like a people magnet for the leader.

Clear and competent communication is vital for the quality leader. When communication is plagued by poor grammar, an unclear message, poor timing, or ineffective delivery, it reflects negatively on the credibility of the leader and the organization.

Each of these demonstrates a leader's skill and sincerity, whether from the lectern, talking to individuals, or leading the human resources within the institution. Without a focus on each of these areas, the academic leader loses executive credibility.

Executive Credibility
Scriptural Basis & Devotional

Leaders with Executive Credibility can accurately discern risks and rewards, choose reliable solutions, and clearly explain their plans to constituents. Executive Credibility is a measure of our sincerity and skill with people. Sincerity comes from the heart, but skills can be sharpened and improved. By adding QM values and methods to your routines, people will gain confidence in your leadership, especially when you take time to listen and give competent answers.

When people know that we are who we say we are and that we will be just and fair in the conduct of our business, they are more likely to cooperate with us. But if a person's integrity or wisdom is in doubt, people will express their feelings in ways that are detrimental. To grow in influence, we must demonstrate emotional maturity as well as competence because when a person is perceived to be "kind, honest and fair, his kingdom stands secure" (Proverbs 20:28 [TLB]).

In Isaiah 42: 1-4 (NIV) the writer speaks prophetically of Jesus:

> *Here is my servant, whom I uphold, my chosen one in whom I delight; I will put my Spirit on Him and He will bring justice to the nations, He will not shout or cry out, or raise His voice in the streets. A bruised reed He will not break, and a smoldering wick He will not snuff out. In faithfulness He will bring forth justice; He will not falter or be discouraged until He establishes justice on the earth.*

Leaders who are growing in these attributes will invoke the greatest confidence in the constituency that forms around them. They will function under the grace of the Spirit of God, not shouting, crying out, or raising their voices. They will not be eager to break off or snuff out the value of another person's contribution. And they will not falter or become discouraged until they establish justice where they lead. The implications here go far beyond the administration of work or the judgments that are required to establish equity. This scripture describes an individual who understands how to be an example of justice.

The Hebrew word translated as "justice" is most commonly translated as just or justice, such as in 1 Chronicles 18:14 (NIV):

> *David reigned over all of Israel, doing what was just and right for all his people.*

However, it is also translated as "dimensions, specifications, standards, regulations, ordinances, practices, precepts, requirements, the prescribed way, and the proper time and procedure." It tells us that to faithfully bring forth justice, we must demonstrate the right way to do things in both word and deed.

Executive Credibility Self-Assessment

Using the scoring scale, rate each area of the question. At the end of the Assessment, tally the score by letter (i.e. tally the totals for A, for B, and C, separately).

On a scale of 1 to 5, where 1 is Never, 2 is Hardly Ever, 3 is Some of the Time, 4 is Most of the Time, and 5 is All of the Time,

1) How often is sincerity towards people demonstrated by
    A. Each of the leaders in the organization?
    B. Each of the team members in your area?
    C. You?
2) How often are discussions logical and reasonable by
    A. Each of the leaders in the organization?
    B. Each of the team members in your area?
    C. You?
3) How often is interaction free of manipulation, pressuring, or pushing by
    A. Each of the leaders in the organization?
    B. Each of the team members in your area?
    C. You?
4) How often is communication clear and competent by
    A. Each of the leaders in the organization?
    B. Each of the team members in your area?
    C. You?

	Place your response for each question in the appropriate cell. Total the columns in the "T" row at the bottom.		
	Total of A Leaders in the Organization	Total of B Team Members in your Area	Total of C You
1			
2			
3			
4			
T			

Executive Credibility
Institutional Checklist of To Dos

Incorporate these items into the practice of your institution to engage in this QM Value:

- ☐ Clearly communicate both verbally and in writing (take time to review written communication and think before you speak).
- ☐ Control your emotions (particularly anger).
- ☐ Be sincere with people inside and outside the organization (mean what you say; say what you mean).
- ☐ Discuss topics reasonably (avoiding manipulation, pressure, and personal bias).
- ☐ Sharpen and improve your skills and demonstrate by doing the work right.
- ☐ Develop and maintain good working relationships.

Executive Credibility Reflection

5

Personal Authenticity

Personal Authenticity
Definition & Discussion

With the value of personal authenticity, we move into the personal values of the quality manager. To be personally authentic is to be credible and real, basing decisions on facts instead of conjecture and not false, phony, or fraudulent. Personally authentic individuals are people of integrity. They are not duplicitous in their actions, saying one thing and doing another. They live by what they hold to be true.

When leaders are personally authentic, they are who they say they are. They are transparent in their dealings with customers, coworkers, and others. I recently watched as a friend went through a situation that ended in a divorce. Those of us close to them were stunned. The individual had kept an abusive situation quiet for years. As we reflected on it, they had always been secretive in their interactions, not letting others know about their real person. We had never known the real person. What they said was not what they did.

Another category of people who lack personal authenticity often are referred to as snake-oil salesmen. They are shady and shifty. You always expect they have some trick up their sleeve.

The auto industry is rife with examples of those who lack personal authenticity, from used car salespeople to mechanics who try to fool the unknowing into paying for repairs they do not need. When you find one who is credible and real, you will gladly pay for the quality you receive.

In higher education, we would hope that leaders reflect personal authenticity. As academics we are supposed to be delivering Truths (with a capital T) about the fields of study at our institution.

I once worked with a college where a leader lacked personal authenticity. As we worked together, it became clear that he could not be trusted. To protect my integrity, I alerted my supervisors when there were discrepancies. One discrepancy, in particular, related to this leader seeking payment for classes he did not teach, which ultimately led to his termination. I recently saw this person at a conference where it appeared he was trying to negotiate a deal with a group of service organizations. I felt guarded and doubtful about this man. I remembered his earlier lack of integrity and could not help but question his motives years later.

Personal authenticity is vital for the faculty member as well. Imagine an instructor who lacks personal authenticity and is grading a subjective assignment. Imagine not having enough integrity to use credible information when preparing course materials. Imagine not connecting well with students because the professor refuses to be authentic with them. Students may dutifully sit through class, but real learning will be lost . . . except for the negative example of how not to do it.

Our personal authenticity affects both our work life and our personal life. If we fail to be a consistent person of integrity who has personal authenticity, we will fail in all areas. When we cannot be trusted because we lack personal authenticity, it makes our leaders and/or followers lose faith in us and lowers our relevance.

When the message and actions move beyond what is real and credible and are not based on fact, the message is tarnished. For an institution that is supposed to be faith-based, a tarnished message tarnishes the gospel.

Personal Authenticity
Scriptural Basis & Devotional

The aim of our charge is love that issues from a pure heart and a good conscience and a sincere faith.
I Timothy 1:5 (ESV)

Personal Authenticity is a measure of our resolve to live a consistent life. It is an indicator of the sensitivity of our conscience and how obediently we respond to the conviction of the Holy Spirit. True accountability begins in the recesses of the heart, where our hidden will and desires are tested by our knowledge of the will of God. The choices we make to discipline our souls, bring consistency to our words and deeds, and obey the Lord, are the ultimate proof of our credibility.

One of the dictionary definitions of faith is fidelity (or faithfulness) to one's promises; something that is believed with strong conviction as a system of religious beliefs. A classical Greek definition of faith is to be "morally persuaded of the truth." The success we experience as leaders and ethical change-agents will greatly depend on how morally persuaded we are about the need for change and then how faithfully we model the values and principles of our management doctrine. But the most emotionally challenging test for us as leaders is to live consistently with those things we are morally persuaded are true and right, even if the decisions we make affect people's motivations or livelihood in a negative way.

As leaders, we are obligated to empower the promises we make by keeping the fire of the Zero Defects heart attitude (discussed later) burning brightly. An essential element for "fanning the flame" is getting it right on the decisions we make. But the more important question is, "How can we know our information is reliable?" Simply put, reliable methods produce reliable results.

Personal Authenticity is at the heart of every leader's credibility, whether it is in a spiritual role that is intended to model his or her faith, in a job description based on business or science competencies, or, as is more likely, a real-world demand for both. The faith we need to make a personal decision spiritually or as a workplace leader springs from the same source of values and facts that carry us to the place of being morally persuaded that what we have decided is "true and right." This is consistent with the dictionary definition of "wisdom" which is "knowledge of what is true and right coupled with good judgment."

Personal Authenticity Self-Assessment

Using the scoring scale, rate each area of the question. At the end of the Assessment, tally the score by letter (i.e. tally the totals for A, for B, and C, separately).

On a scale of 1 to 5, where 1 is Never, 2 is Hardly Ever, 3 is Some of the Time, 4 is Most of the Time, and 5 is All of the Time,

1) How often is authenticity demonstrated by
    A. Each of the leaders in the organization?
    B. Each of the team members in your area?
    C. You?
2) How often is integrity demonstrated by
    A. Each of the leaders in the organization?
    B. Each of the team members in your area?
    C. You?
3) How often are decisions reliable and fact-based as made by
    A. Each of the leaders in the organization?
    B. Each of the team members in your area?
    C. You?
4) How often is transparency demonstrated by
    A. Each of the leaders in the organization?
    B. Each of the team members in your area?
    C. You?

	Place your response for each question in the appropriate cell. Total the columns in the "T" row at the bottom.		
	Total of A Leaders in the Organization	Total of B Team Members in your Area	Total of C You
1			
2			
3			
4			
T			

Personal Authenticity
Institutional Checklist of To Dos

Incorporate these items into the practice of your institution to engage in this QM Value:

- ☐ Walk with integrity personally and expect it of your team.
- ☐ Keep a clear conscience about your actions.
- ☐ Base decisions on facts that are given due diligence to be proven.
- ☐ Set accountability systems in place with people that care for your well-being.

Personal Authenticity Reflection

6

Ethical Dependability

Ethical Dependability
Definition & Discussion

Ethics is a common conversation in our culture today. We see examples of poor ethics in companies like Enron, Equifax, Wells Fargo, and many others. This has created a distrust of businesses worldwide, including colleges and universities. Problems with for-profit higher education institutions come to mind.

Ethical dependability is a key piece of the quality manager's practice. The ethically dependable manager is seen as trustworthy in practical matters and reliable in his or her dealings with finances and people.

One would expect a faith-based institution to be Biblically centered and free of ethical issues, but that is not always true. Ethical dependability has taken a beating in the Christian higher education from recruiters painting a rosier picture of how classes will work to cases of embezzlement where leaders used the institution as their personal slush fund.

In Christian colleges, idolatry and fear-based leadership can be real issues. "Follow me as I follow Jesus" may be the theme those lacking in ethical dependability share with students and other constituents while the leaders are living a distorted and sinful life. Leaders are only slightly off target can still lead followers in a wrong direction.

For the prospective student trying to decide whether to attend a Christian educational program, ethical dependability is vital. Here are some examples where ethical dependability is lacking:

- When a leader speaks "evangelistically" to his or her board sharing the accomplishments over the year, the board may be surprised and ill-equipped to assist when downturns happen.

- Then there are the times when an institution broadcasts an inflated picture. One Christian institution announced publicly that it was having "record enrollment." Speaking to leaders, I learned the institution actually was down in enrollment and trending downward. This was confirmed based on evidence of layoffs.

- When a rosier picture of what it takes to be successful is given, students may expect they will not need to study effectively because the work will be easy or that they can maintain their very busy lifestyle without giving up anything. One recruiter I knew had this problem. It was an awkward situation. The institution had outsourced its recruiting to a third party and the recruiter worked for that third party. The recruiter was supposed to be a Christian but was regularly found to be giving information that students wanted to hear to get them in the program. The third party did not want to release the recruiter because she was bringing in students and making them money. The institution could not remove her because it was not her employer.

- Earlier we discussed a leader's lack of transparency to the board, but the opposite also happens where the board is not being ethical towards the leader. While a board may not be "in the weeds" of the day-to-day operations, it also needs to operate with ethical dependability. When a board fails to act appropriately, either through lack of understanding or a reticence to take ownership, the board fails in its ethical dependability. In speaking with a colleague, he said when an institution fails and closes, it is primarily due to the actions or inactions of the board. Sadly, many board members are not prepared for the hard work of their position.

Quality managers are known for being honest and direct in their dealings. There are not shades of gray when dealing with ethically dependable individuals.

For organizations desiring to test the ethical dependability of team members, the key is to start out with limited amounts of authority and limited amounts of money. Team members, in this sense, include: new hires, new responsibilities in current roles, or coaching an employee who previously failed at a task. By starting with small amounts, the organization can determine whether team members can be faithful with authority or money before giving them more responsibility. Team members then have opportunity to develop a proven track record. This starts from the top, at the board level. When developing a path to the board, have potential board members serve on advisory boards to give evidence of their faithfulness. With a new leader reporting to the board, test him or her in small matters first.

One institution recently had its leader indicted and subsequently convicted. The reaction of potential students has been clear: they do not trust the school. As a result, the school continues to drop in enrollment and it is unclear if it will survive this scandal.

Ethical Dependability is a vital aspect for individuals and an organizational culture that reflects ethically dependable individuals will gain a stellar reputation. However, when that reputation is tarnished due to low ethics, it is a long battle to regain trust.

Ethical Dependability
Scriptural Basis & Devotional

Even a child makes himself known by his acts, by whether his conduct is pure and upright.
                    Proverbs 20:11 (ESV)

One who is faithful in a very little is also faithful in much, and one who is dishonest in a very little is also dishonest in much.
                    Luke 16:10 (ESV)

Ethical Dependability is a measure of our trustworthiness in practical matters. It is an indicator of the confidence that others have that we will be honest, fair, and faithful. These qualities are critical in a leader if people are going to rely on a leader to make good decisions. These qualities are essential not only in our personal life and family, but also to the success of any career or ministry. If you want to be trusted, you should strive to develop reliable ethics and good judgment.

Who among us has not said, "I would like to do that all over again with what I now know?" When we look back at how things could have been, we can see how some important decisions were affected by our character. Greed, passion, or the personal need for power may have caused us to say "yes" to a risky idea when a more secure, disciplined person would have declined. Or careful and prudent analysis could have helped us properly evaluate the ethics of a business relationship that would later prove to be unsavory.

There might also have been times when fear of failure or our questionable judgment neutralized us and left us unable to take advantage of reasonable opportunities when they occurred. As we gain experience in life, we can begin to figure out what did or did not work for us and decide how things can be done better in the future. When these reflective times reveal problems with our values and strategies, they become opportunities "for acquiring a disciplined and prudent life" and "doing what is right and just and fair" (Proverbs 1:3).

A person's value system operates like a program in a computer. It is a complex set of interrelated ideas, learned experiences, and personal theories through which information is processed, analyzed, and output as actions to be taken. It includes all the values and strategies we have collected over our lifetime along with the various priorities we have assigned them. When we have to make a decision, this program with all its preset ideas and concepts (good and bad, accurate and inaccurate) begins to converge so we can decide the correct action to take and the strength with which it should be executed. Changing the viewpoint of just one item in our program to a more reliable perspective can have enormously positive effects.

People need a consistent role model for the actions and values being requested before they will trust someone and respond to him or her properly. Without it, people will either refuse to follow their leader or will cooperate for the wrong reasons, such as fear, idolatry, or intimidation. The influence that character has on good judgment and behavior cannot be minimized. It is the real issue behind many of the failures that occur at home and at work. In fact, reliable character is a person's most important asset.

We begin to shape our character early in life as we learn the principles that will become the foundation for our values and strategies. They include the significance of truth, what is just and fair, the difference between responsible and irresponsible actions, respect for the rights and property of others, the need for compassion and faithfulness in relationships, and how to exercise moral restraint. Everything else we learn or do is affected by these fundamentals.

As leaders, it is our role to develop those fundamentals in our children, students, team members, and followers. Those fundamentals can be developed steadily throughout life or throughout the relationship by starting with small opportunities and graduating to larger opportunities to demonstrate ethical dependability. Those "faithful in little" who successfully and successively show their faithfulness will learn to be "faithful in much."

Ethical Dependability Self-Assessment

Using the scoring scale, rate each area of the question. At the end of the Assessment, tally the score by letter (i.e. tally the totals for A, for B, and C, separately).

On a scale of 1 to 5, where 1 is Never, 2 is Hardly Ever, 3 is Some of the Time, 4 is Most of the Time, and 5 is All of the Time,

1) How often is a high ethical standard demonstrated by
    A. Each of the leaders in the organization?
    B. Each of the team members in your area?
    C. You?
2) How often is reliability with money demonstrated by
    A. Each of the leaders in the organization?
    B. Each of the team members in your area?
    C. You?
3) How often is honesty and directness demonstrated by
    A. Each of the leaders in the organization?
    B. Each of the team members in your area?
    C. You?
4) How often is trustworthiness demonstrated by
    A. Each of the leaders in the organization?
    B. Each of the team members in your area?
    C. You?

	Place your response for each question in the appropriate cell. Total the columns in the "T" row at the bottom.		
	Total of A Leaders in the Organization	Total of B Team Members in your Area	Total of C You
1			
2			
3			
4			
T			

Ethical Dependability
Institutional Checklist of To Dos

Incorporate these items into the practice of your institution to engage in this QM Value:

- ☐ Develop systems for developing the ethical dependability of team members starting small and growing the responsibility of team members.
- ☐ Develop ethical conversations into your curriculum for students.
- ☐ Measure and test for ethical dependability as part of your institutional assessment practice by assuring that performance keeps the promise to constituents.
- ☐ Review your systems and staffing to reduce risk from an ethical perspective.
- ☐ Review communications to constituents to assure that they tell the truth in a direct, straightforward manner.
- ☐ Keep track of office supply levels as a means of measuring for ethical dependability.

Ethical Dependability Reflection

7

KTP Culture

KTP Culture
Definition & Discussion

KTP stands for Keeping the Promise and refers to the type of mindset required in quality management. As quality managers, we must work to keep the promises we make to coworkers, clients, constituents, and students. To extend that, we as leaders need to help our culture embrace this mindset.

At the heart of a KTP Culture is mutual respect, accountability, and professionalism. When leaders show mutual respect, they are helping to promote the accomplishment of the organization. Even when disagreements arise, mutual respect keeps them from turning into wars that tear away at the organization.

It is exceptionally refreshing when I begin working with a client to find this culture largely in place. When the leader chooses to be accountable to the board and shows mutual respect and professionalism to his or her team, it is a strong foundation on which to begin developing new initiatives. I want to be around those types of leaders to learn how they work for my own professional development. . .as their consultant! Imagine what that culture does for a team member who works and lives in it daily. Even when things go wrong, there is growth because the respect and professionalism provide a learning opportunity instead of condemnation.

Alternatively, I have also worked with organizations that failed in this area. Instead of an environment that promotes learning and growth through respect and professionalism, you have a range of outcomes when things go wrong and even when things go right. There is fear of the repercussions, backstabbing, undercutting, slander, and a number of other environmental maladies in a race to the top. Ironically, this race often ends up leaving the individual and institution in a heap on the metaphorical floor.

Accountability may be a dirty word to some because it seems to limit freedom. When we set boundaries and remain accountable both to mutually-agreed-upon boundaries and to each other, we get a freedom that allows us to run without always worrying about risk of doing wrong. The child who is accountable to his parents by staying in the yard knows he is free of getting hit by a car from playing in the street.

Accountability in a higher education institution should be absolutely central in the practice due to our need to accomplish the mission, vision, and institutional, departmental, program, and course outcomes. Our assessment processes should be about accountability and learning from what we have done in our practices.

When a standard of professionalism is set in the culture, there is a known quantity by which to measure. A friend of mine owns his own insurance agency and has a "no jeans" policy except for specific times. When pressed on the policy, he tells people that this is a standard of professionalism to honor customers. At a university where I worked, married individuals were not allowed to ride with members of the opposite sex alone. That standard of professionalism honored the sanctity of marriage and protected both individuals.

In higher education, our level of professionalism has a direct effect on our constituents. When donors see a high level of professionalism, they seek to support that and see the institution grow. When board members see the level of professionalism is high in an organization, they work to keep it high, giving their due diligence to their duties as board members. When new team members see the professionalism, they want to be part of and contribute to an institution that has that environment. When students see professionalism demonstrated, they not only learn to be that way in their future practices but feel cared for as a student (and that often turns them into donors in the future).

The KTP culture, founded on these qualities, needs to be stated in your organizational values and empowered by the actions of the leader. Without willingness to state the values and actually practice them, the culture cannot be established.

One of my favorite quotes about culture is attributed to Peter Drucker and Mark Fields (and slightly modified by Bill Aulet). Setting the culture is vital and KTP is a strong way to do it.

> *Culture eats strategy for breakfast, technology for lunch, and products for dinner, and soon thereafter everything else too.*

At every level, higher education organizations need a KTP culture. Keeping the promise to every constituency in every way possible is what makes an organization growth-ready.

KTP Culture
Scriptural Basis & Devotional

While KTP culture is the goal, each of us will likely experience tyranny at some time in our life. Because Proverbs 25:26 tells us that a person who yields to tyranny is like a "muddied spring or a polluted well," it is very important to know what to do, especially at work, while we wait upon the deliverance of the Lord. Here are some suggestions:

1) Do not be afraid. "The fear of man brings a snare, but he who trusts in the Lord will be exalted" (Proverbs 29:25 [NAS]). Jesus said,

> *I tell you friends, do not be afraid of those who can kill the body and after that can do no more. But I will show you whom you should fear. Fear him who, after the killing of the body, has power to throw you into hell. Yes, I tell you fear him. Are not five sparrows sold for two pennies? Yet not one of them is forgotten by God. Indeed, the very hairs of your head are numbered. Don't be afraid; you are worth more than many sparrows.*
> Luke 12:5-7 (NIV)

2) Unless you are asked to do something illegal or immoral, obey your earthly masters in everything. Keep doing your job, and do it, not only when their eye is on you and to win favor, but with sincerity of heart and reverence for the Lord.

> *Whatever you do, work at it with all your heart, as working for the Lord, not for human masters, since you know that you will receive an inheritance from the Lord as a reward. It is the Lord Christ you are serving.*
> Colossians 3:22-24 (NIV)

3) Be prepared to hold your superiors accountable without trying to exercise authority or influence you do not have. All that is required is that you speak the truth humbly. Remember,

> *God has not given us the spirit of timidity, but of power, love and discipline [or sound judgment].*
> 2 Timothy 1:7 (NAS)

4) Be prepared to make an investment of suffering. Tyrants and the people around them do not like being told they are wrong. Proverbs 29:16 (TLB) says,

> *When rulers are wicked, their people are too; but good men will live to see the tyrant's downfall.*

Just remember,

> *Who is there to harm you if you prove zealous for what is good? But even if you should suffer for the sake of righteousness, you are blessed. Do not fear their intimidation, and do not be troubled, but sanctify Christ as Lord in your heart, always being able to give an account for the hope that is in you, yet with gentleness and reverence. Keep a good conscience so that in the thing in which you are slandered, those who revile your good behavior in Christ may be put to shame. For it is better, if God should will it so, that you suffer for doing what is right rather than for doing what is wrong.*
> 1 Peter 3: 13-17 (NAS)

Effective leaders often describe how they take time to look honestly into their own hearts and minds and answer this simple two-part question: How much fear and insecurity do

I actually have about the work I do? And how can people in my workspace positively or negatively affect the outcomes of my efforts? Healthy introspection can lead to important discoveries about who we are and why we say and do the things we say and do. And what usually follows is opportunity for improvement. Personal and professional success is related to what we can do to change—to learn and grow—so our performance measures continue to push the envelope of excellence. We can improve through self-analysis and introspection, through feedback from our working environment, or through a combination of both. But one thing is certain, managers and leaders are either improving to build a better tomorrow or slowly deteriorating in a false equilibrium of "activity disguised as achievement."

KTP Culture
Self-Assessment

Using the scoring scale, rate each area of the question. At the end of the Assessment, tally the score by letter (i.e. tally the totals for A, for B, and C, separately).

On a scale of 1 to 5, where 1 is Never, 2 is Hardly Ever, 3 is Some of the Time, 4 is Most of the Time, and 5 is All of the Time,

1) How often is a sense of mutual respect demonstrated by
    A. Each of the leaders in the organization?
    B. Each of the team members in your area?
    C. You?
2) How often is accountability to others demonstrated by
    A. Each of the leaders in the organization?
    B. Each of the team members in your area?
    C. You?
3) How often is a standard of professionalism demonstrated by
    A. Each of the leaders in the organization?
    B. Each of the team members in your area?
    C. You?
4) How often is value of the work of the organization connected to fulfilling constituent requirements and needs demonstrated by
    A. Each of the leaders in the organization?
    B. Each of the team members in your area?
    C. You?

	Place your response for each question in the appropriate cell. Total the columns in the "T" row at the bottom.		
	Total of A	Total of B	Total of C
	Leaders in the Organization	Team Members in your Area	You
1			
2			
3			
4			
T			

KTP Culture
Institutional Checklist of To Dos

Incorporate these items into the practice of your institution to engage in this QM Value:

- ☐ Identify the promises that you make to your constituencies.
- ☐ Identify the promises that you should be making to your constituencies.
- ☐ Develop accountability relationships within your practice.
- ☐ Discuss and enforce practices of professionalism that your organization will keep.
- ☐ Show mutual respect to colleagues above, beside, <u>and</u> below your role.
- ☐ Remove gossip as an option in your organization.

KTP Culture Reflection

8

Zero Defects Attitude

Zero Defects Attitude
Definition & Discussion

Just what is this "Zero Defects Attitude" anyway? Some may think that defects only apply to products. Others might hear "zero defects" and think no mistakes are allowed. Neither is the case. The Zero Defects Attitude (ZDA) is *not* about having *no* mistakes or errors in practices, procedures, services, and products of the individual or organization.

ZDA is a heart attitude that the quality manager holds. It is a sense of pride in the workmanship he or she delivers. Rather than focusing on perfection, which is impossible given our fallen nature, the focus of ZDA is never allowing an error or mistake to be "acceptable." ZDA inherently works to keep the promise to others. An attitude to remove defects from products and services always has the promise made as its focus.

You may think this is a semantic argument between allowing some mistakes and not accepting them as "okay." Some strands of quality management allow for a statistical degree of error in their processes, products, and services because they know mistakes will be made. Unfortunately, that method simply sanctions the incompetence that leads to errors and mistakes rather than preventing them.

For example, how many flies are acceptable in your burger? Unless you are into eating bugs, your answer is probably "zero." To keep the promise to the client, the quality manager is not going to accept even one fly in the burger. If one is found, the quality manager will make it right for the customer. In doing so, the quality manager continually works to avoid errors and mistakes. That silly example is fairly benign, albeit gross.

Let us take the principle further, though. What if a tire company has an acceptable level of error in the production of tires? What if a flawed tire causes the car to go out of control and overturn when you are driving 75 miles per hour, in traffic, and with small children in the car? Is that an acceptable level of error?

While you may not deal with such immediate life-or-death errors, you may be dealing with issues that have long-term implications. What if you deliver a degree program that is poorly designed, poorly taught, and expensive? Students exit your institution with potentially higher student debt and a degree that has not prepared them for the market. What if your lack of ZDA causes you to condone a poor hiring process that results in a sexual predator on your team? What if you turn people off to the message of the gospel because you failed to have sound educational practices? These are very real issues.

Dangerously, we often give ourselves a pass working in Christian higher education because our *intentions* are good. Our "goodness" is a trait that we think carries us and allows us to coast a bit. Goodness or good intentions are not enough. Just meaning well and leaving it at that falls short of the Zero Defects Attitude. When a mistake or error occurs, a person with a Zero Defects Attitude will make it right immediately so that it does not happen again.

A Zero Defects Attitude is important regardless of the field and affects every area of personal and professional practice. Higher education is no exception. Our errors and defects are often imprinted on the hearts and minds of our students and constituents. As leaders in higher education, our calling is important, and we must take the steps to ensure that we do not accept defects in our offerings. We must do better, and a Zero Defects Attitude helps us do that.

Zero Defects Attitude
Scriptural Basis & Devotional

I press on toward the goal to win the prize for which God has called me heavenward in Christ Jesus. All of us, then, who are mature should take such a view of things. And if on some point you think differently, that too God will make clear to you. Only let us live up to what we have already attained.
Philippians 3: 14-16 (NIV)

The idea of "pressing on towards the goal to win the prize" is the concept of Zero Defects Attitude. We will likely have some victories in this life. A runner that wins the race has victory. However, the moment that we stop pressing towards the goal of the prize, the moment the runner stops training to win the race, is the moment that we stop improving and expecting to win.

The foundational concept of Biblical "personal growth" (mentally, emotionally, and spiritually) as a follower of Christ has its own parallel metric in the professional life of a believer. Our desire to learn and grow both personally and professionally is an indicator of how much we understand about "what we have already attained" in Christ and whether or not we are preparing to become "salt and light" to the people who interact with us and observe our life at work.

Personal credibility is directly linked to the competence and maturity we display in the execution of our duties in the workplace and a Zero Defects Attitude helps us execute those duties effectively. Whether we work as a leader or as a faithful servant to others in authority, our grasp of the essential vocational elements sometimes projects just as clearly to unbelievers that we are acting within a higher level of self-discipline and personal accountability than is the norm in the workplace. In other words, a Zero Defects Attitude improves what I grew up calling my "witness" to others around me. When we establish our understanding of defects as based on Biblical standards, how much more are we aligning our witness to others with a Zero Defects position.

Zero Defects Attitude
Self-Assessment

Using the scoring scale, rate each area of the question. At the end of the Assessment, tally the score by letter (i.e. tally the totals for A, for B, and C, separately).

On a scale of 1 to 5, where 1 is Never, 2 is Hardly Ever, 3 is Some of the Time, 4 is Most of the Time, and 5 is All of the Time,

1) How often is the constituent the focus of the work done by the organization as demonstrated by
    A. Each of the leaders in the organization?
    B. Each of the team members in your area?
    C. You?
2) How often is a sense of satisfaction about the work done by the organization (or pride of workmanship) demonstrated by
    A. Each of the leaders in the organization?
    B. Each of the team members in your area?
    C. You?
3) How often are promises kept by
    A. Each of the leaders in the organization?
    B. Each of the team members in your area?
    C. You?
4) How often are errors, mistakes, and problems accepted as "okay" by
    A. Each of the leaders in the organization?
    B. Each of the team members in your area?
    C. You?

	Place your response for each question in the appropriate cell. Total the columns in the "T" row at the bottom.		
	Total of A Leaders in the Organization	Total of B Team Members in your Area	Total of C You
1			
2			
3			
4			
T			

Zero Defects Attitude
Institutional Checklist of To Dos

Incorporate these items into the practice of your institution to engage in this QM Value:

- ☐ Review your policies, procedures, systems, and practices for errors and defects and correct them.
- ☐ Review your personal practices for errors, defects, and resting in your own "goodness" and correct them.
- ☐ Review your work for areas where you are proud of your accomplishments and develop principles for good practice.
- ☐ Continue to evaluate your entire practice to make sure that you keep the promise to your constituencies.

Zero Defects Attitude
Reflection

Assessment Review & Reflection

Once you have completed each of the assessments in previous chapters, follow these steps:

1) Copy the totals lines for each area to the corresponding line in the table below.
2) Add each of the columns in the Totals row. Each cell has a maximum of 20 points so the Total amount should not exceed 160.
3) Calculate the percentage in the bottom row for each column by dividing the Total Amount by 160 and multiplying by 100.

	Leaders in the Organization	Team Members in your Area	You
Vocational Certainty			
Process Quality			
Administrative Consistency			
Executive Credibility			
Personal Authenticity			
Ethical Dependability			
KTP Culture			
Zero Defects Attitude			
Total			
%			

Reflection Questions

Now that you have scores calculated, reflect on them to understand how each group did. Consider each of the areas below as you reflect:

Evaluate your Rankings. The first question to ask about the scores above: Are they a fair reflection of each group (leaders, team members, and you)? Were you too hard or too soft in your responses? Do not spend too much time considering this but make sure you were not flippant in your responses or overly easy or hard on one particular group due to a personal bias.

Evaluate the Differences. As you see the numbers in one place, how do the differences strike you? Are there differences between your score and the leaders or members of your team that stand out? If so, why do you think there are those differences? Is there a disconnect between your values and theirs?

Evaluate the Deficiencies. Review each category for each group. Are there specific areas where any of them fell considerably short of the potential total? Why? How do you think they could improve?

Record your reflections below in the notes section.

Assessment Reflection

Next Steps

Now that you have completed this Quality Management Checklist, there are opportunities to continue your personal, academic, and organizational development in the area of quality management through Progressus Education Services and InterLearn. Because you have completed this devotional, we will discount the price.

Progressus (www.ProgressusEd.com) is an education-based service organization that helps organizations and individuals develop their quality management practices through training and consulting services. We offer a Certified Quality Higher Education Leader certification through our affiliate partnership with the Quality Management Institute (QMI). The certification is offered with education leaders in mind.

Through this training, you will be able to see:

- Excellent leadership of human resources leading to reduced staff turnover.
- Effective management of the budget and financial matters of your institution.
- Forward leaning structuring of operational systems for more effective engagement of constituents and community.
- Stronger board and student relationships that lead to more effective accomplishment of the mission and vision of your institution.
- Systematic practices for organizational leadership.
- Relating reasonably and competently to the business community members represented in your institution's area with the personal and organizational capacity to offer them valuable, Biblically-consistent counseling and training.

This certification process will include an online, flipped classroom model that is self-paced. Additionally, there are discussion groups available with the leaders of QMI and Progressus that will help you think through the material as it relates to your personal and academic practice. We will also coach you through a project that demonstrates your knowledge base of the QM principles. The cost of this certification program at the time of printing is $2,195 per person. Because you have completed this inventory, QMI and Progressus are offering a 15 percent discount on the course. That makes the course $1,866.

In addition to the certification training, Progressus goes a step further. We work with organizations to help them implement the quality management principles they have learned in the training into their institutions to help them achieve optimal quality. We start with a quality systems review to assess your current status and where we can help the most. Then we help you implement the processes, procedures, and changes that will bring your organization growth through quality measures. Because we are mindful of size and scope, we can work affordably with small or large organizations.

InterLearn (www.InterLearnEd.com) is a higher education consulting firm focused on helping institutions with adult and online programming. Our primary focus is developing curriculum for online programming. As part of that work, we partnered with QMI to create a for-credit version of the Quality Management Certification program that is 12-semester-hours in length. Your institution can offer this programming, along with other online programming options, to your students. They would have academic credit and a field-based certification from QMI upon successful completion.

For more information on our certification process or implementation services, please contact us through one of the methods below:

Telephone:	(918) 895-1185
e-mail:	jfischer@progressused.com or
	jfischer@interlearned.com

www.ingramcontent.com/pod-product-compliance
Lightning Source LLC
Chambersburg PA
CBHW071402290426
44108CB00014B/1653